Steadwell Books World Tour
NICARAGUA

ADRIANA DOMINGUEZ

Raintree

Chicago, Illinois

Copyright Permissions
Raintree
100 N. LaSalle
Suite 1200
Chicago, IL 60602
Customer Service 888-363-4266
Visit our website at www.raintreelibrary.com

Library of Congress Cataloging-in-Publication Data
Dominguez, Adriana.
  Nicaragua / Adriana Dominguez.
      p. cm. -- (World tour)
Includes bibliographical references and index.
  ISBN 0-7398-6814-4 (library binding-hardcover)
  1. Nicaragua--Description and travel--Juvenile literature. 2. Nicaragua--Social life and customs--Juvenile literature. I. Title. II. Series.
  F1524.D58 2004
  972.85--dc21

                              2003006077

Printed in the United States of America
10 9 8 7 6 5 4 3 2 1   08 07 06 05 04

Photo acknowledgments
Cover (top) Buddy Mays/Corbis; (bottom, L-R) J. Chandler/WINS, Brent Winebrenner/ImageState

Title page (L-R) Buddy Mays/Corbis, Buddy Mays/Corbis, Kevin Schafer/Corbis; contents page (L-R) Alan Cave/DDB Stock Photo, Nik Wheeler/Corbis; pp. 5, 41 Larry Luxner; p. 7 Archivo Iconografico, S. A./Corbis; p. 9 Wally McNamee/Corbis; p. 12T Bettmann/Corbis; p. 12B Gary Braasch/Corbis; pp. 14, 15T, 25 Alan Cave/DDB Stock Photo; p. 15B Mario Lopez/AP Wide World Photos; pp. 16, 18, 34 Nik Wheeler; p. 21L Skip O'Rouke/The Image Works; p. 21R J. Chandler/WINS; pp. 22, 37 Darwin Vivas; pp. 23, 33, 43T Buddy Mays/Corbis; p. 24 Brent Winebrenner/Photri Inc.; pp. 27, 42T Nik Wheeler/Corbis; p. 28 Bob Kalman/The Image Works; p. 29 Brian Vikander; p. 31L Brent Winebrenner/ImageState; p. 31R Kevin Schafer/Corbis; p. 35 Janet Moran/Heinemann Library; p. 36 Javier Galeano/AP Wide World Photos; p. 39T Chris Barton/chrisbartonphotos.co.uk; p. 39B Science VU/NSDC/Visuals Unlimited; p. 40 Yoram Kahana/Shooting Star Int.; p. 42B Owen Franken/Corbis; p. 43B Norman Owen Tomalin/Bruce Coleman Inc.; p. 44T Ruben Dario Museum; p. 44C Mark Duncan/AP Wide World Photos; p. 44B Carraro Mauro/Corbis SYGMA

Photo research by Amor Montes de Oca

CONTENTS

Welcome to Nicaragua

Are you planning a trip to Nicaragua, or do you just like learning about different countries? Nicaragua is a very interesting place. It is called "The Land of Lakes and Volcanoes" because it has the two largest lakes in Central America and eleven active volcanoes. That's quite a lot for such a small country! There is plenty more to learn about Nicaragua. This book will tell you about its history, food, people, and much more. Are you ready to take a tour? Read on!

Tips to Get You Started:

• *Use the Table of Contents*

In this kind of book, there may be some sections that interest you more than others. Take a look at the Contents. Pick the chapters that interest you and start with those. (Check out the other chapters later.)

• *Use the Glossary*

When you see **bold** words in the text, you can look them up in the Glossary. The Glossary will help you learn their meanings.

• *Use the Index*

If you are looking for a certain fact on Nicaragua, then you might want to go to the Index. There you'll find a list of all the subjects covered in the book and the pages they can be found.

▲ **LUSH AND GREEN**
The western half of Nicaragua is made up mostly of valleys separated by low but rugged mountains and many volcanoes. This is a view of the mountains and Lake Nicaragua.

Do you know where the name Nicaragua comes from? Reading about this country's history will give you the answers to this and many other questions.

Early History

Footprints that are 6,000 years old were discovered under layers of volcanic ash in Nicaragua. They belonged to Native Americans called Acahualincas. Not much is known about these early Nicaraguans. However, we do know that by the 900s, **indigenous** people from Mexico began to migrate into western Nicaragua.

When the Spanish arrived in western Nicaragua, they found three main tribes: the Niquirano, the Chorotegano, and the Chontal. Nicaragua's name comes from the name of the chief of the Niquirano tribe, Nicarao. Explorer Christopher Columbus spotted Nicaragua in 1502, but it wasn't until 1524 that Spain sent its first successful expedition into the country. This expedition was led by Francisco Fernández de Córdoba. He founded the cities of Granada and León. This began the **Colonial** Period, the period during which the Spanish began to colonize, or move to, Nicaragua.

During the Colonial Period, much of the native population died from diseases brought over by the Europeans. Many of the survivors became slaves to the Spanish. About 200,000 of them were shipped off to work in the gold mines of Peru and to other parts of Spain's empire. Of the 1 million people who lived in western Nicaragua before the Spanish arrived, only 11,000 were left by 1548. This period lasted for nearly 300 years.

◄ **CHRISTOPHER COLUMBUS**
Christopher Columbus was born in 1451 in Genoa, Italy. He died in 1506 in Valladolid, Spain. He spotted Nicaragua's Miskito Coast from his ship while sailing past the country.

Independence

On September 15, 1821, Nicaragua, Honduras, El Salvador, Costa Rica, and Guatemala joined together to declare their independence from Spain. Together, the countries formed the Central American Federation. This was such an important event that Nicaragua continues to celebrate Independence Day on September 15. In 1838, the provinces' union **dissolved** and Nicaragua was declared a free, self-ruling nation.

Nicaragua Today

In the 20th century, many people continued to fight for control over Nicaragua because of its location on the Pacific Ocean. Many turbulent years followed, and the country went through some troubled times. The United States even controlled the country by force from 1912 to

1933. A Nicaraguan peasant army, headed by Augusto César Sandinoa, led a **rebellion** against the United States that lasted from 1926 to 1933. Once the United States left the country, the Somoza family ruled Nicaragua by force for 40 years. In 1979, a group that called itself the **Sandinistas** started a **revolution** that eventually defeated the Somoza government.

Free elections were held in 1984. Daniel Ortega Saavedra, a candidate from the Sandinista party, won the election, but problems continued. A group called the **Contras** wanted to remove the Sandinistas from power. In 1986 an international scandal that became known as the Iran-Contra Affair let the world know about the United States' involvement in Nicaragua. Then-president Ronald Reagan confirmed that the United States had been selling **arms** to a Middle Eastern country named Iran to help finance the Contras' efforts in Nicaragua. This became a scandal because the United States Congress had promised not to intervene with Nicaragua's affairs anymore. Additionally, Iran was an enemy of the United States during that time, and was known to support terrorist groups who kidnapped United States citizens.

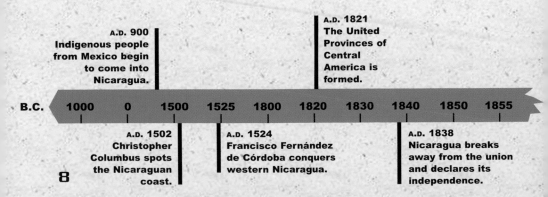

A.D. 900
Indigenous people from Mexico begin to come into Nicaragua.

A.D. 1821
The United Provinces of Central America is formed.

B.C. 1000   0   1500   1525   1800   1820   1830   1840   1850   1855

A.D. 1502
Christopher Columbus spots the Nicaraguan coast.

A.D. 1524
Francisco Fernández de Córdoba conquers western Nicaragua.

A.D. 1838
Nicaragua breaks away from the union and declares its independence.

8

▶ **LIEUTENANT CORPORAL OLIVER NORTH**

Marine Lt. Col. Oliver North was one of the central figures in the plan to secretly sell arms to Iran, against U.S. law.

In 1989 **free elections** were held, and Nicaraguans regained hope for a better future. But by then the country had seen much violence and its people were very poor.

In 1996, Arnoldo Alemán was elected. Enrique Bolaños Geyer replaced him in the 2001 elections. Recently, President Geyer discovered that ex-president Arnoldo Alemán stole about $100 million from his country during his presidency. This news of government **corruption** shows that Nicaragua's problems continue, but the country is taking steps in the right direction and trying to make it a better place to live and visit.

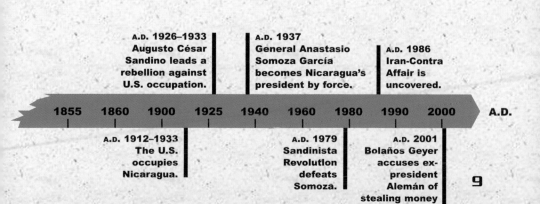

A.D. 1926–1933
Augusto César Sandino leads a rebellion against U.S. occupation.

A.D. 1937
General Anastasio Somoza García becomes Nicaragua's president by force.

A.D. 1986
Iran-Contra Affair is uncovered.

| 1855 | 1860 | 1900 | 1925 | 1940 | 1960 | 1980 | 1990 | 2000 | A.D. |

A.D. 1912–1933
The U.S. occupies Nicaragua.

A.D. 1979
Sandinista Revolution defeats Somoza.

A.D. 2001
Bolaños Geyer accuses ex-president Alemán of stealing money from Nicaragua.

9

A LOOK AT NICARAGUA'S GEOGRAPHY

Nicaragua is the largest country in Central America. Central America is the strip of land that connects North and South America. Its territory covers 49,998 square miles (129,494 sq km) of land and sea.

Land

Nicaragua can be divided into three major regions: the Pacific lowlands, the Caribbean lowlands, and the central highlands. The Pacific lowlands in the west are flat except for a string of active volcanoes between the Gulf of Fonseca and Lake Nicaragua. Western Nicaragua sits on a fault line, or a series of "cracks," on the earth's crust. These cracks are the reason there is so much volcanic activity in this area. Volcanic eruptions are very good for the soil because they provide it with a lot of minerals, making it very **fertile**.

The Caribbean lowlands in the east make up about half of the country. The area is made up of tropical rain forests and pine savannas. A rain forest is a place where trees and plants grow tall and close together—and of course, it rains a lot! A pine savanna is an open space where most of its few trees are pine trees. The Caribbean lowlands are commonly called the Miskito Coast, after the people who live there. Between the Pacific lowlands and the Caribbean lowlands are the central highlands. This is where you can find the highest mountains in Nicaragua. The tallest one is named Pico Mogotón. It is 6,900 feet (2,103 m) tall.

▶ NICARAGUA'S SIZE

Nicaragua covers an area of 49,998 square miles (129,494 sq km), and is slightly smaller than the state of New York. It is bordered by Costa Rica to the south, and Honduras to the north.

U.S.A.

MEXICO

NICARAGUA

SOUTH AMERICA

BELIZE

GUATEMALA

HONDURAS

EL SALVADOR

NICARAGUA

NICARAGUA
★ National Capital
● Major Cities
— Rivers

0   25   50 Miles
0   25   50 KM

Managua ★
Rivas ●

Lago de Nicaragua

Bluefields ●

COSTA RICA

► EARTHQUAKE!
This picture shows the destruction in Managua caused by the 1972 earthquake.

Water

Nicaragua has the first and second largest lakes in Central America. Both of them are in the western part of the country. The largest is called Lake Nicaragua. It covers an area of 3,100 square miles (8,000 sq km). There are over 350 islands in Lake Nicaragua, leading people to say that there is an island for every day of the year. The lake is connected to the Caribbean Sea by the San Juan River, which is why so many people have

◄ SAN JUAN RIVER
This historic river was the stage for great battles between the Spanish empire and British and French pirates during Nicaragua's Colonial Period.

NICARAGUA

★ National Capital
— Rivers

Caribbean Sea

Rio CoCo

Rio Wawa

Rio Kurinwás

Managua ★

Lago de Nicaragua

Pacific Ocean

Rio San Juan

wanted to use Nicaragua as a trade route to the Pacific. The second largest lake in Nicaragua and Central America is Lake Managua. It covers an area of 405 square miles (1,050 sq km). Lake Apan is in the central highlands. It is not as large as the other two, but it provides hydroelectricity for almost the entire country. Hydroelectric power comes from dams that harness the energy of falling water to generate electric power.

There are plenty of beaches in Nicaragua. Since the country sits between two coasts, all you have to do is choose between the Pacific Ocean and the Caribbean Sea! If you like to swim, you may also want to check out one of the many **crater** lakes in the west. You don't get to swim in a crater very often!

Weather

Nicaragua's climate varies according to altitude, or how high above sea level an area is. The coastal areas are always very hot. The average temperature in those areas is 81°F (27°C). Bring plenty of tee-shirts! If the heat is not for you, head for the central highlands. It is cooler there because the area sits higher above sea level. Temperatures there range between 60° and 80°F (16° and 27°C). No matter where you go, don't forget to bring an umbrella! The rainy season is very long in Nicaragua. It begins in May and does not end until November. You might need a sturdy umbrella if you decide to visit the Caribbean coast during the rainy season. Rainfall there can measure up to 100 inches (254 cm) in a season.

▲ FORTRESS OF SAN PABLO
This fortress, located on the shores of Lake Nicaragua, was built in the mid-1700s. It was designed to protect the city of Granada against dangerous pirates.

◄ LITTLE CORN ISLAND
Located 45 miles (72 km) off the eastern shore of Nicaragua, Little Corn Island is inhabited by roughly 750 people who earn their living from lobster fishing. It is a popular vacation spot for tourists.

▲ NICARAGUAN RAINSTORM
These children are walking down a flooded street in the city of Managua after a heavy rain.

GRANADA: A BIG-CITY SNAPSHOT

▲ **GRANADA—NICARAGUA'S TOUGHEST CITY!**
Having survived several pirate attacks and twice
being almost burned to the ground, the city of
Granada is now a popular tourist destination. It
was established in 1524 by the Spanish conqueror
Don Francisco Hernández de Córdoba.

Granada is one of the oldest cities in the Americas and
is one of Nicaragua's biggest tourist attractions. A visit to
Granada is a must for anyone traveling to Nicaragua.

Main Facts

Granada is in the western part of Nicaragua. It was founded in 1524 on the shores of Lake Nicaragua near Mombacho Volcano. The city takes its name from a city of the same name in Spain. It is located 27 miles from the capital city of Managua.

Main Attractions

Granada is a beautiful city, full of churches and buildings built by the Spanish during the Colonial Period. As you walk around, stop by the handicraft stores that you will find along the way. Handicrafts are traditional items made by local people, such as ceramic sculptures and hammocks, among others. They make unique gifts for your friends back home.

The Parque Central (Central Plaza) is a very active place to visit. It is surrounded by the city's cathedral, City Hall, and cultural center. There is a beautiful outdoor café in the plaza, so you will certainly want to return there when it's time to relax and have a snack.

From there, you should walk over to the Convento de San Francisco. This convent was built in 1529. It is Granada's first church and is one of the oldest buildings in Central America. Inside the convent you will find statues made by the indigenous people of Nicaragua.

Getting tired yet? If your feet are becoming a little weary, you can rent a bicycle. If you don't feel like pedaling, hail a horse-drawn carriage. They are Granada's version of taxicabs.

◀ **PARQUE CENTRAL**
In the heart of Granada
is the Parque Central.
Here you can enjoy some
local delicacies, listen to
traditional music, or sit and
take in the architecture.
This cathedral is in the
center of Granada and
faces the Parque.

Lake Nicaragua and Isletas

The city is very hot, so you probably won't mind getting a bit closer to the water. Granada sits on the shore of the largest lake in Nicaragua. The only freshwater sharks in the world live in Lake Nicaragua! You may not be able to see sharks from the shore, but you will probably notice the isletas, or small islands. There are 350 of them, all created by volcanoes. There are many boats that can take you to visit the islands, and if you enjoy swimming or fishing, these are a great spot for both!

Mombacho Volcano

You will notice Mombacho Volcano as soon as you arrive in Granada. It's hard to miss! You can hike to the top of its crater with a guide and enjoy a breathtaking view of the city of Granada. On your way back down from the volcano, you might want to take a tour around the hot springs and the tall-grass canal found at the volcano's base.

GRANADA'S TOP-10 CHECKLIST

☐ Take a ride through the city in a horse-drawn carriage.

☐ Visit the Convento de San Francisco Museum and look at traditional indigenous sculptures.

☐ Rent a bike and enjoy sight-seeing. Enjoy the beautiful architecture from the Colonial Period.

☐ Go swimming or fishing in Lake Nicaragua.

☐ Visit Granada's cathedral.

☐ Relax at one of the cafés by the Parque Central.

☐ Buy local handicrafts for friends and family back home.

☐ Hire a guide and hike up Mombacho Volcano.

☐ Take a tour of the hot springs at the base of Mombacho Volcano.

☐ Rent a boat and visit one of the many islands in Lake Nicaragua.

4 TOP SIGHTS

There is a lot to see in Nicaragua. Here are some suggestions that will help you experience some of the best sites the country has to offer.

Masaya

Masaya is a town located 16 miles from Managua. It sits on the edge of a volcanic crater lake under Masaya Volcano. The city is famous for its traditional handicrafts. You can find leather goods, large hammocks, tapestries, embroidered dresses, carved masks, jewelry, and even rocking chairs there. The best place to buy crafts is in one of the open-air stalls that make up the Mercado de las Artesanias, or Arts and Crafts Market. The Arts and Crafts Market holds a festival every Thursday evening called Vamos a Masaya (Let's Go to Masaya). The festival is a good way to enjoy the best of Nicaraguan music and traditional food.

Are you a history buff? Masaya was a base for **Sandinista** rebels during the **Revolution.** If you like history, the city offers a wonderful opportunity to learn more about Nicaragua's battles. The Museum and Gallery of Heroes and Martyrs shows the role the people in Masaya played in the Sandinista Revolution.

Before leaving the area, you should visit the volcano that shares its name with the city. The volcano is part of the Masaya Volcano National Park. Since the crater is still active, the view from its rim should be unforgettable. You can see and smell gas and steam burst up from far below the earth's crust. Be careful, and take lots of pictures!

▼ MASAYA OPEN AIR MARKET

In 1978, the Nicaraguan National Guard set fire to the original market square in an attempt to destroy a place where revolutionaries supposedly gathered. It has since been rebuilt and is very popular with tourists and residents.

▲ MASAYA VOLCANO

Masaya is the most active volcano in Nicaragua. The Spanish first described the volcano in 1524. Since then, Masaya has erupted at least 19 times.

FASCINATING FACT

There is something at the top of the Masaya volcano that you probably would not expect: a wooden cross, erected by Spanish explorers. Some say that the Spanish raised it to try to stop the natives from tossing people into the crater as a sacrifice to the god of fire. Others say that the Spanish thought that the volcano was possessed, so they erected the cross to cast away the evil spirit. The cross continues to stand on the same spot today!

Managua

Managua is Nicaragua's capital city. It is located in the western part of the country, on the southern coast of Lake Managua and around the beautiful Tiscapa Lagoon. Managua is the largest city in Nicaragua, so there's a lot to see and do there. If you walk on Bolívar Avenue, you will eventually reach Managua's cultural center. There, you can visit the Central Park, the Plaza of the Republic, the ruins of the Santiago Cathedral, the National Cultural Palace, and the new President's House. You can also visit the National Museum, the National Library, and many other cultural centers and museums. Near the National Cultural Palace you will find the Cultural Center of Managua. The Center has many traditional arts and crafts on display.

Also near this area is the Rubén Darío National Theatre. It was named after a world-famous Nicaraguan poet. There, you will have a chance to see the beautiful Rubén Darío fountain, made out of carved marble.

▶ **TISCAPA LAGOON** Located between the old and new sections of Managua, Tiscapa is one of six lagoons that surrounds the city.

In Managua, you can also see some 6,000-year-old Acahualinca footprints showcased in the Las Huellas de Acahualinca Museum. The footprints are the most important **archaeological** find in Nicaragua.

After visiting all of these interesting places, you may feel a little tired. Go to the top of the Tiscapa Hill, relax, and enjoy a great view of Managua and the nearby volcanoes. If possible, go at sunset when the view is the most beautiful. You can also relax by the second largest lake in Nicaragua, Lake Managua.

Like other cities popular with tourists, Managua has many arts and crafts markets. You should visit some of them. Even if you don't want to buy anything, you will have a chance to look at the beautiful work of local artists. The city also hosts two great festivals that make it come alive: the Youth and Music Festival (in March) and the Agostina Celebration (in August). If you happen to be there during those times of the year, enjoy!

The Miskito Coast

The Caribbean Coast on Nicaragua's eastern side, known as the Miskito Coast, covers about 50 percent of the entire country. Very few people live in this area of lowland rain forest. Most of the ones that do are groups of Miskitos, Sumus, and Ramas. The Miskitos are a mix of the indigenous Bawihka people of northeastern Nicaragua and runaway African slaves from the British Caribbean territories. As a result of being the largest group in the area, the Miskitos began to control smaller indigenous groups, such as the Sumu and the Rama. Unlike most of Nicaragua, the British controlled and protected this region centuries ago. Because of this, many people here speak a mixture of English and their own native languages, instead of Spanish.

If you'd like to go to this fascinating part of the country, you will have to join a tour. Most of them are ecotours. Ecotours are tours that take visitors into undeveloped areas to see the beauty of nature. These types of tours are becoming quite popular in Nicaragua. The tours offer transportation, lodging, and guidance through the wild landscape. You will not find many of the comforts from home there, but you will definitely find adventure!

Just getting there will be an experience you won't forget. The roads to the coast are rugged and few. One of them will take you from Matagalpa to Puerto Cabezas. A better road will take you from Managua to Rama in the south. The rest of the journey to the city of Bluefields on the Caribbean Sea takes place on a boat along the beautiful Escondido River. Once you reach the Caribbean coast, you can go fishing in lagoons, snorkel in the coral reefs, or lie on long, white, deserted beaches. After all of this traveling, you'll need the rest!

▲ CARIBBEAN COAST
While this section of Nicaragua is popular with tourists, it is also one of the poorest regions in the country.

Mark Twain, the author of Tom Sawyer, sailed the San Juan River, which flows from Lake Nicaragua all the way into the Caribbean Sea. Before Twain, a British admiral named Horatio Nelson also sailed the river. Nelson fought the Spanish before surrendering to them at El Castillo, an old fortress that still stands.

León

The city of León is located 55 miles (90 km) north of Managua. Like Granada, the original city of León was founded in 1524 by Francisco Hernández de Córdoba. But an earthquake destroyed it in the early 1600s. The León of today was constructed after the earthquake. If you would like to see the remains of "Old León" you can visit its ruins. They are only 20 miles (30 km) south of "new" León.

There are many beautiful colonial buildings to see in León. The first place you should visit is the cathedral. It is the largest colonial building in Central America. On your way in, you will see six large lions decorating the entrance and the fountain in the church square. Once inside, you will find many beautiful paintings.

On your way out, look under the arches of the cathedral. There you will find the tomb of Rubén Darío, one of the greatest Nicaraguan poets. Darío was born in León in 1867. If you would like to learn more about this poet, you can visit the house where he grew up. It is now the Rubén Darío Museum. If you're lucky, you have chosen to visit León during one of its religious celebrations. The León Cathedral hosts important religious ceremonies that turn into huge parties, fireworks and all!

Do you like the heat? If you do, head over to the Hervideros de San Jacinto! The Hervideros are hotbeds that are connected to the Telica Volcano. They're only 13 miles (22 km) from León. The Telica Volcano heats up an underground river that shoots hot water and mud up through the Hervideros' holes. The mud is believed to have **medicinal** qualities. It may be hot there, but the shooting mud will be fun to watch!

▲ LEÓN CATHEDRAL
The Metropolitan Cathedral located in the city of León is considered the largest cathedral in Central America. It was built over a 60-year period during the 16th and 17th centuries and has 11 altars inside.

GOING TO SCHOOL IN NICARAGUA

◄ RURAL SCHOOLING These girls in rural Nicaragua are studying for a math exam, using the side of a house as a chalkboard.

Before 1980, only 57% of Nicaraguans could read and write. In 1980, the Sandinista government launched a national **literacy** program. Many people who had never before gone to school learned to read and write. During this time, schools were established in the most rural areas. Literacy rates reached 87% by 1985.

But in the 1990s, literacy rates fell again. Today, many Nicaraguan children who are enrolled in elementary school rarely attend. Only 51% of Nicaraguans attend high school. Illiteracy is once again becoming a big problem in Nicaragua.

By law, Nicaraguan children go to school when they are six and stay in school for six years. But many of them do not stay in school through the sixth grade. Children who come from poorer families often have to leave school to help their parents earn money by selling candy, tortillas, or water in the streets, or by working in the fields. This prevents them from going to school and getting a good education.

One popular Nicaraguan sport is well-loved in the United States as well—baseball! Most communities have a baseball field where even the poorest children can learn to play the game using a stick for a bat and a rolled-up sock for a ball. The country has several professional baseball teams. The largest baseball stadium is in Managua, and seats 4,000 people. It was renamed Estadio Dennis Martínez, to honor the first Nicaraguan baseball player to ever make it into the American Major Leagues. Nicaragua's national baseball team came in fourth in the 1996 Olympic Games.

Some of the other sports that are popular in Nicaragua are volleyball, basketball, cycling, and soccer. In a country surrounded by water, you can expect water sports to be popular as well. You can go fishing in either of the two large bodies of water that border the country, and in its many lakes, rivers, and lagoons. Surfing is very popular on both the Pacific coast and in Lake Nicaragua, where windy areas create very large waves.

▶ **DENNIS MARTÍNEZ STADIUM**
Dennis Martínez won more baseball games than any other Latin American pitcher. His nickname in Nicaragua is "El Presidente."

FROM FARMING TO FACTORIES

Ever since the Spanish arrived, Nicaragua's economy has depended on the **exportation** of farm products. Coffee became a major crop in the 1840s, but natural disasters and increased competition from other countries have caused problems for this crop in Nicaragua over the years. Cotton, sugar, bananas, and cattle have also been important to the country's **economy.**

Shrimp and lobster are farmed and exported, and tuna, bass, and mackerel are caught off the country's Pacific shores. But a hurricane nearly destroyed the fishing industry in 1988. The industry eventually recovered, but in 1992 a tidal wave crashed over the Pacific coast and devastated the area. Many of the fish production factories were destroyed. Production had recovered by 1997, but another hurricane destroyed the industry once again in 1998. It will now probably take many years for Nicaragua's fishing industry to recover a third time.

Just as it did in the past, **agriculture** remains the most important part of the country's economy. Of all of Nicaragua's people, 42% still work on farms today. They are either hired by local farm owners or travel to areas where they can find work. The service industry also has a strong workforce, employing 38% of Nicaraguans in restaurants, hotels, and places where they serve other people.

Less than 15% of Nicaraguans work in manufacturing or factories. Major industries include cement, chemicals used for farming, petroleum products, metal processing, beer, soft drinks, and food processing. Nicaragua also has

▼ **LOBSTERS!**
Lobster fishing is a popular livelihood for Nicaraguans living on the coast.

▲ **MATAGALPA, NICARAGUA**
While this region is known for its coffee growing, many tourists visit Matagalpa because of its cool climate and pretty countryside.

sugar refineries, small **textile mills**, and coffee-processing plants that produce instant coffee. But these factories only make enough products to meet the needs of local Nicaraguans. That means that Nicaraguans import, or buy from other countries, more things than they produce. This makes it difficult for the country's economy to get better, since Nicaraguans have to spend more than they earn. It also makes it difficult for the country to improve the lives of its people.

THE NICARAGUAN GOVERNMENT

Nicaragua is a republic, where citizens vote for members of the government. Nicaraguans can legally vote at age 16. Like the United States, Nicaragua's government is made up of three branches called the executive, legislative, and judicial branches. Elections of executive and legislative members of government take place every five years.

The executive branch is made up of the president, the vice president, and the cabinet. The president and vice president are elected by the people. The cabinet is a group of people the president chooses to help him or her make laws. The executive branch makes sure those laws are obeyed. The legislative branch is made up of 90 members of the National Assembly. The National Assembly makes the laws, approves budgets, elects Supreme Court judges, and has the power to **veto** the president's decision made by the president through a majority vote. The judicial branch is made up of judges, including those on the Supreme Court. The judicial branch makes sure that laws are fair.

NICARAGUA'S NATIONAL FLAG

The flag of Nicaragua has three bands: the bottom and top bands are blue, and the middle is white. The white stripe stands for Central America's position between two oceans, which are represented by the two blue stripes.

RELIGIONS OF NICARAGUA

About 85% of Nicaraguans are Catholic, which is a type of Christianity. Christians follow the teachings of Jesus as written in the Bible, their holy book. The history of Nicaragua's Catholicism dates as far back as 1524, when the first Catholic church was built in the city of Granada by Spanish conquerors.

About 10% of Nicaraguans are Protestant. Protestantism is another form of Christianity. Unlike the Catholic faith, Protestants do not follow the **pope**. The majority of the Protestant churches in Nicaragua are Pentecostal, but there are other **sects** as well, such as Moravians, Baptists, and Seventh-day Adventists. Some indigenous Nicaraguans still follow their traditional spiritual practices. These practices usually concentrate on the natural world and worship objects found in nature.

Most of Nicaragua's Jewish population left the country after the Sandinista government closed their only synagogue in 1979 and began persecuting them. Some Jews returned after the Sandinista government left in 1990, but today, the Jewish population of the entire country consists of fewer than 50 people.

NICARAGUAN FOOD

Many people in Nicaragua make their food from "scratch." Cooks often grind their own corn to make tortillas, for instance. Nicaraguans take their time when they make their food and eat it. A Nicaraguan meal is usually a family affair. Lunch is their main meal and can last for over an hour. While it might seem strange that people can fit such a long and large meal at noon into work and school schedules, this is very common in Latin America.

When you sit down to eat a meal in Nicaragua, rice and beans will definitely be on the menu. These two basic ingredients can be found in most Nicaraguan dishes. Corn tortillas are also common, and delicious! They are commonly used in dishes such as quesillos, which is a tortilla filled with soft cheese and onions.

Another very popular dish is nacatamales. Nacatamales are made with potatoes, pork, tomatoes, rice, onions, and spices, mixed in a dough and wrapped in a banana leaf.

You can wash down all of this great food with a great Nicaraguan drink, a fresco. It is fruit juice mixed with water and (almost always) a bit of sugar.

▶ **FRIED CHEESE, ANYONE?**
This woman is serving some fried cheese in this market in Masaya. This is a popular local side-dish.

Nicaraguan Recipe

GALLO PINTO (SPECKLED ROOSTER)

Ingredients:
2 tablespoons of vegetable oil
2 medium-size onions, sliced
    thin
2 cups of precooked red beans
1 cup of uncooked white rice

WARNING:
Never cook or bake by yourself. Always have an adult assist you in the kitchen.

Directions:

Put 1 cup of rice and 2 cups of water in a pot and boil, uncovered, at medium heat. Once it boils, turn the heat down to medium-low. Place the lid on the pot, keeping it tilted to allow steam to escape. When you can see holes or "craters" in the rice, put the lid on tight. Turn the heat to low. Simmer for another 10 minutes. Now the rice is ready.

Heat the vegetable oil in a heavy pot. Cook the onion in the oil until it turns golden. Add the precooked beans and the cooked rice and continue to stir for about 10 minutes. That's it! You have made the basic gallo pinto recipe.

You might have noticed that the basic recipe does not actually contain rooster. Why the name then? The name actually comes from the "speckled" appearance of the mixture.

◀ SAN CRISTÓBAL VOLCANO
A child walks in a field that is covered in mud and ash in Valle de Managua. The people in this region must constantly be alert for volcanic activity.

Nicaragua is rightly called "The Land of Lakes and Volcanoes." Overall, there are about 58 volcanic peaks throughout the country. Many of them are not active, and some of their craters are filled with water, which has turned them into huge, beautiful lagoons. Most of the active volcanoes can be found in the western part of the country. There are about 11. These belong to a chain of volcanoes called the Marrabios Range.

Active volcanoes can be dangerous when they erupt. Occasionally, their ash can reach very far distances. Nicaragua has a variety of volcanoes, including some that are very large, some that are unusual, and some that are very **temperamental!** Here's a few of them:

The San Cristóbal Volcano is the largest volcano in Nicaragua. It is located about 87 miles (140 km) northeast of Managua. It is 5,725 feet (1,745 m) high. Although San Cristóbal is a very tall volcano, it also seems to be a very quiet one. Its first reported eruption took place in 1520 and has kept itself pretty quiet, until recently. At the beginning of 2000 and again in May of 2001, the volcano released small amounts of ash. This has people a little bit puzzled. Has the great San Cristóbal awakened from its long rest?

Cosigüina Volcano is not one of the volcanoes in the western range. Instead, it forms a large **peninsula** that extends into the Gulf of Fonseca. The volcano is 2,860 feet (872 m) high and very beautiful. In 1835 Cosigüina was the source of a short but very powerful eruption. Ash from the volcano fell as far away as Mexico, Costa Rica, and Jamaica!

▶ **APOYEQUE VOLCANO**
This unique volcano is located on the Chiltepe Peninsula. Its crater consists of a beautiful green lagoon. Apoyeque's last eruption occurred 4,000 years ago.

Telica and Cerro Negro are two of Nicaragua's very active volcanoes. Eruptions from Telica were reported as long ago as the 1500s. Its highest point measures 3,480 feet (1,061 m). Boiling mud pots called Hervideros de San Jacinto (San Jacinto's Hotbeds) are connected to Telica Volcano. The Hervideros are a very popular tourist destination. Locals often take mud from the hotbeds and sell it for its medicinal qualities. Cerro Negro is Central America's youngest volcano. It was born in April 1850, and has since been one of the most active volcanoes in Nicaragua. Because heavy amounts of ash have fallen from the volcano and damaged crops and buildings in the area, not many people live near Cerro Negro.

The Concepción and Maderas Volcanoes sit on Ometepe Island in Lake Nicaragua. Concepción is the larger of the two, and also the most active. In the past 100 years, Concepción has erupted 24 times. The last time was in 1986. Its frequent eruptions have actually increased the height of the volcano in the past few years. Maderas Volcano is much quieter than its neighbor. There is no recorded time for its last eruption. In addition to the volcanoes, Ometepe Island houses more than 80 species of birds, mantled howler monkeys, white-faced capuchin monkeys, sloths, deer, and many other animals, including snakes and lizards. So, as you can see, a visit there is a must!

▶ **VOLCANOES ON OMETEPE ISLAND**
Ometepe Island is the largest island in the largest lake (Lake Nicaragua) in Central America. Ometepe is made up of two volcanoes, Concepción and La Madera.

▲ **CERRO NEGRO VOLCANO**
Cerro Negro has erupted at least 20 times since 1850. The longest eruption was in 1960 and lasted 3 months!

HOLIDAYS

▶ **LA PURÍSIMA**
This festive celebration can be traced back to 7th century Spain.

Nicaraguans celebrate many Catholic holidays. *Semana Santa* (Holy Week) is one of the most important, and most people do not work during that entire week. Christmas Eve and Easter are also very important Catholic holidays. Each town and city in Nicaragua honors its own patron saint on a specific day of the year. This is a person the Catholic Church honors for living a good life and doing something very special, by making them a saint.

Nicaraguans also celebrate a special holiday on December 7 and 8 called La Purísima. This holiday celebrates the Immaculate Conception of the Virgin Mary. During this holiday, each family builds an altar inside the house and keeps the door open so that people on the street can see it. Guests are given Purísima presents, which are sweets or some other small gift.

Nicaragua's Independence Day falls on September 15. It commemorates Central America's independence from Spain, which was declared in 1821. Another important national holiday is Labor Day, celebrated on May 1.

LEARNING THE LANGUAGE

English	Spanish	How to say it
Hello	Hola	OH-la
Good day	Buenos días	BWAY-nahs DEE-ahs
Goodbye	Adiós	ah-dee-OHS
My name is...	Me llamo...	MAY YAH-mo
Thank you	Gracias	GRAH-see-ahs
You're welcome	De nada	DAY-nah-da

QUICK FACTS

NICARAGUA

Capital ▶
Managua

Borders
Honduras (N)
Costa Rica (S)
Caribbean Sea (E)
Pacific Ocean (W)

Area
49,998 sq miles
(129,494 sq km)

Population
5,023,818

Literacy Rate
70% of all Nicaraguans
can read and write

◀ **Largest Cities**
Managua (1,146,000)
León (164,300)
Chinandega (129,100)
Masaya (118,000)
Granada (95,200)

Longest River
Coco River
466 miles (750 km)

▲ Flag of Nicaragua

Chief Crops
Coffee, bananas, sugarcane, cotton, rice, corn, tobacco, sesame seeds, soybeans, beef, veal, pork, poultry, dairy products

Coastline ▶
505 miles (910 km)

Major Industries
Food processing, chemicals, machinery and metal products, textiles, clothing, petroleum refining and distribution, beverages, shoes, wood

Natural Resources
Gold, silver, copper, tungsten, lead, zinc, timber, fish

◀ Monetary Unit
Córdobas

PEOPLE TO KNOW

◀ RUBÉN DARÍO

Rubén Darío is the country's best-known poet. He lived from 1867 to 1916. His poetry had such a big impact on the rest of Latin America that he became known as the prince of Spanish-American literature. If you visit the city of León, you will find this important national figure's tomb resting beneath the arches of the city's huge cathedral.

▶ DENNIS MARTÍNEZ

Dennis Martínez was born in Granada on May 14, 1954. Nicknamed "El Presidente" (The President), he holds the baseball record for the most games won by a Latin-American pitcher. President Arnoldo Alemán renamed Managua's national stadium in honor of Martínez, because he was the first Nicaraguan to play in the American major leagues.

◀ BARBARA CARRERA

Barbara Carrera was born in Managua on December 31, 1945. She began modeling at the age of 17, but is probably best known for her role in the 1983 James Bond film *Never Say Never Again*. Today, Barbara continues to work in television and film; she recently guest-starred in the TV show *That '70s Show.*

MORE TO READ

Want to know more about Nicaragua? Check out the books below.

Malone, Michael R. *A Nicaraguan Family*. Minneapolis: Lerner Publishing Group, 1998.

This book tells the story of a Nicaraguan family who fled their country in 1979 to become refugees in the United States and begin a new life in Miami, Florida.

Riehecky, Janet. *Nicaragua*. Mankato, Minn.: Capstone Press, 2002.

This book will give you more information about the geography, animals, food, and culture of Nicaragua.

Chambers, Catherine. *Volcanoes*. Chicago: Heinemann Library, 2000.

Read more about these sometimes violent forces of nature, like the ones that dot the landscape of Nicaragua.

GLOSSARY

Agriculture—the practice of growing crops and raising livestock

Archaeological—from archaeology. Archaeology studies the remains of a culture that no longer exists.

Arms—any kind of weapon

Colonial—anything made by Europeans during the time period when they were building colonies

Contra—meaning "against" in Spanish, the word was used to name the group of armed rebels who were "against" the Sandinista government and wanted to overthrow it by force

Corruption—wrongdoing by a person or government

Crater—a large hole in the earth, such as that of a volcano

Dissolve—to break up or fall apart

Economy—a country's industry, trade, and finances

Exportation—selling goods to another place or country

Fertile—something that is very productive. When soil is fertile, it is strong enough to grow large amounts of plants or fruits

Free election—an election in which the citizens of a nation can vote for their members of government

Indigenous—the first people to live in a specific place

Literacy—knowing how to read and write

Medicinal—something that is used to cure disease or ease pain

Peninsula—a portion of land partially surrounded by water but is still connected to a larger body of land

Pope—the leader of the Roman Catholic Church

Rebellion—an armed battle against the government

Revolution—a battle to try to change a country's government

Sandinistas—a group of rebels who defeated the Somoza government and created their own in its place. They were named after General Augusto César Sandino, who led a peasant army to victory against the United States between 1926 and 1933.

Sect—a group within a particular religion that has its own set of beliefs and follows its own practices

Temperamental—having a moody and unpredictable personality

Textile mills—factories where cloth or fabrics are woven or knitted

Veto—a power of one branch of government to stop another branch of government from carrying out a law or action

INDEX